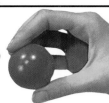

## SCIENCE WORKSHOP

# SHAPES
## STRUCTURES AND MATERIALS

Pam Robson

**A WATTS BOOK**

LONDON NEW YORK SYDNEY

Design              David West
                    Children's Book Design
Designer            Steve Woosnam-Savage
Editor              Suzanne Melia
Picture Researcher  Emma Krikler
Illustrators        Ian Moores
                    Ian Thompson
Consultant          Bryson Gore

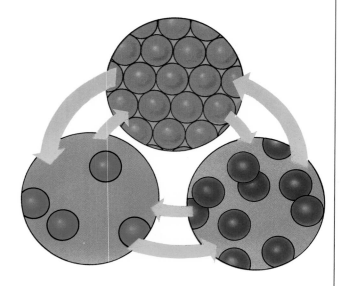

© Aladdin Books Ltd 1993
Created and designed by
N. W. Books
28 Percy Street
London W1P 9FF

First published in
Great Britain in 1992 by
Franklin Watts Ltd
96 Leonard Street
London EC2A 4RH

ISBN 0 7496 1445 5

# CONTENTS

## PHOTOCREDITS

All the photographs in this book are by Roger
Vlitos apart from pages; 6 top, 26 top, 30 top:
Spectrum Colour Library; 12 top, 14 top:
Frank Spooner Pictures; 16 top, 18 top:
Science Photo Library

# INTRODUCTION

From the atoms that form the smallest molecule to the iron girders that support the tallest skyscrapers, structures, shapes and materials are an important part of our everyday lives. The natural world teaches us how to make the best use of materials and shapes to build efficient structures, and by joining shapes made from different materials, we can build a range of structures suited to specific purposes. Throughout history, technological advances have been linked to the discovery of new materials. For example, we refer to the Stone Age, the Bronze Age and the Iron Age in history. The 19th century was the age of steel and the 20th century may well be remembered as the 'Plastic Age'. Some of our greatest technological achievements have been inspired by nature. Scientists are still trying to reproduce a fibre that is as strong as a spider's silk. And if we are to continue to learn from the natural world, we must learn to conserve our planet's resources.

Introduction

Why It Works explaining
science ideas

Bright Ideas
for further
projects

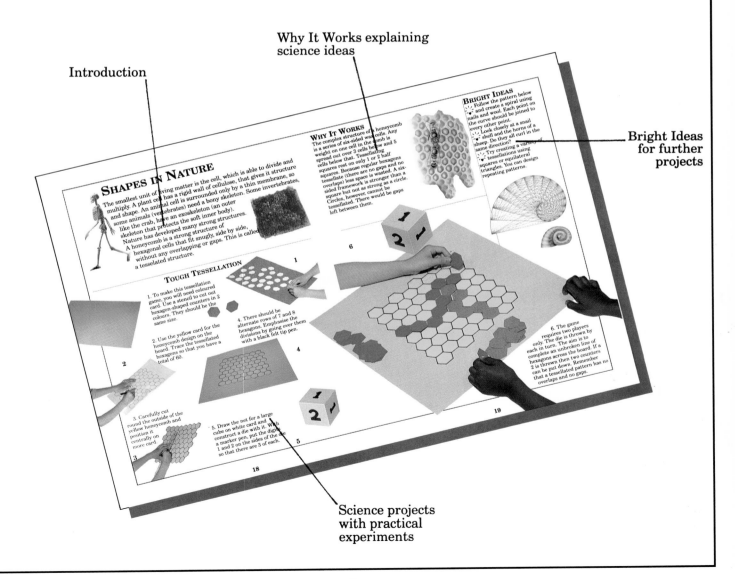

Science projects
with practical
experiments

# THE WORKSHOP

A science workshop is a place to test ideas, perform experiments and make discoveries. To prove many scientific facts, you don't need a lot of fancy equipment. In fact, everything you need for a basic workshop can be found around your home or school. Read through these pages, and then use your imagination to add to your "home laboratory". As you work your way through this book, you should enjoy completing the projects and seeing your models work. Remember, though, that from a scientific point of view, these projects are just the starting point. For example, when you carry out the "Melt Down" experiment on pages 10/11, ask your own questions like "What other materials might heat up quickly?", and so on. Experimenting with equipment, as well as with ideas, will give you the most accurate results.

## MAKING MODELS

Before you begin, read through all the steps. Then, make a list of the things you need and collect them together. Next, think about the project so that you have a clear idea of what you are about to do. Finally, take your time in putting the pieces together. You will find that your projects work best if you wait while glue or paint dries. If something goes wrong, retrace your steps. And, if you can't fix it, start over again. Every scientist makes mistakes, but the best ones know when to begin again!

## GENERAL TIPS

There are at least two parts to every experiment: experimenting with materials and testing a science "fact". If you don't have all the materials, experiment with others instead. For example, if you can't find any fake grass, use green powder paint instead. Once you've finished experimenting, read your notes thoroughly and think about what happened, evaluating your measurements and observations. What conclusions can you draw from your results?

## SAFETY WARNINGS

Make sure that an adult knows what you are doing at all times. Cutting card and wire can be difficult and dangerous if you use sharp scissors. Ask an adult to do this for you. Always be careful with Plaster of Paris, it can be very messy. Never pour unused plaster into the sink. If you spill any water, wipe it up right away. Slippery surfaces are dangerous. Clean up after you have finished.

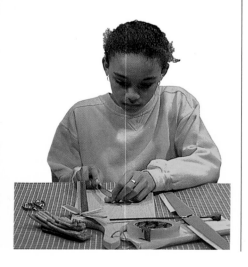

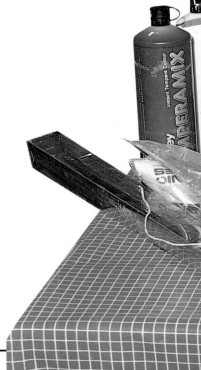

## EXPERIMENTING
Always conduct a "fair test". This means changing one thing at a time for each stage of an experiment. In this way, you can always tell which change caused a different result. As you go along, record what you see. Ask questions such as "why?", "how?" and "what if ?". Then test your model and write down the answers you arrive at. Compare your results to those of your class-mates or friends.

Blanchards
PLASTER OF PARIS
3 KG
NETT WEIGHT
MARTIN & SIMMONDS LTD
TH ROAD LONDON S.E.17

# EARTH'S STRUCTURE

Diamonds are crystals made up almost entirely of carbon. The word crystal comes from the greek 'krystallos', which means 'icy cold', because it was once believed that quartz crystal was permanently frozen into rock. Gemstones crystallise within the Earth's crust, in pockets of molten rock called magma. Magma rises, cools and solidifies, only to be broken up by movements of the Earth's crust and weathering. Then it makes its way back below the surface, to melt once more. Movements of the Earth's crust happen when heat rises from the molten outer core. Molten lava erupts from volcanoes, many of which are still active today.

## COOL CRYSTALS

**1**

1. To grow sparkling crystals, like diamonds, you can use potash of alum crystals. You will also need hot water, a glass jar, a sieve, some string and a pencil. If you would like to grow coloured crystals, just add a few drops of food colouring.

2. Mix 250g of alum into 100ml of hot water in a transparent jar. Be very careful, you must not use boiling water. Stir the alum crystals into the hot water and keep stirring until no more crystals will dissolve.

When you have achieved a saturated solution, leave the jar to stand for about 2 days while the crystals form.

**2**

**3**

3. After 2 days, drain your solution through a sieve to obtain the crystals that have formed.

## WHY IT WORKS

A crystal is a solid body surrounded by flat surfaces. Each identical unit of a crystal has a structural arrangement of atoms (tiny particles). When hot water is added to potassion aluminium sulphate (potash alum), the crystals dissolve. When crystals will no longer dissolve, you have created a saturated solution. Evaporation (loss of water) causes the crystals to re-form as certain atoms in the substance move closer together.

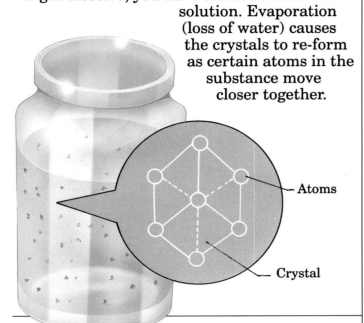

Atoms

Crystal

## BRIGHT IDEAS

☀ Take one of your original crystals and dangle it in your saturated solution once more. Your crystal should grow even larger.

☀ Set up two identical saturated solutions of potash alum. Allow one to cool rapidly by standing the container in ice cold water. Cool the other slowly by standing it somewhere less cold. Observe and time the formation and size of the crystals in each. Keep a record of the fall in temperature of each solution. From the results calculate the actual rate of cooling. Which produces the larger alum crystals?

☀ Try using sugar or magnesium sulphate (Epsom salts) instead of potash alum. You can also use copper sulphate, which is blue, but be careful because it is poisonous. Create a crystalline sculpture by growing your crystals on a shaped pipe cleaner.

**4**

4. Each jar of saturated solution should produce quite a few crystals. You could grow one even larger in some more solution.

# NATURAL STRUCTURES

The effects of weathering, erosion and deposition have created amazing natural structures all over the world. Some rocks are much harder than others; for example, chalk crumbles, but granite is very hard. A waterfall is the result of the erosion of less resistant rock by the river, so that 'steps' of hard rock are left. The Colorado River in North America has shaped the Grand Canyon, one of the world's natural wonders — it is 1200m deep and 320km long. The sea also attacks the land, forcing air into cracks and hurling stones against the cliffs. This erosion creates fantastic arches and stacks (right).

## TRICKLES TO TRIBUTARIES

**1**

1. With a small hacksaw, cut away one of the narrow sides of the tray. Shape the plasticine into small 'rocks' for the bottom of the tray.

3. Now sprinkle the dry sand over the top of the soil. Put most over the highest part of the slope.

**3**

4. By sprinkling some green powder paint over the sand you can create a grassy effect. Position some model trees or bushes across the landscape.

2. Cover the 'rocks' completely with the dry soil. The surface of the soil needs to slope from the back of the tray down to the open front.

5. At this stage, either take a photograph of the landscape or draw a picture. Position the tray on a raised surface with the cutaway end above an empty plastic bowl.

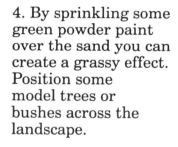

**4**

**2**

**5**

## WHY IT WORKS

The project makes use of soft materials like sand, soil and clay, which are easily eroded. The water behaves like a real river, eroding the top layer of grass before cutting down into the soil and the sand (1). As in the natural world, the lumps of clay in your project resist the flow of the water. The water is forced to take an alternative path around the obstacles (2), forming bends. Eventually, the river changes its course to a more direct path towards the sea, depositing silt, and finally forming a cresent-shaped lake that is cut off from the main stream (3).This is called an ox-bow lake.

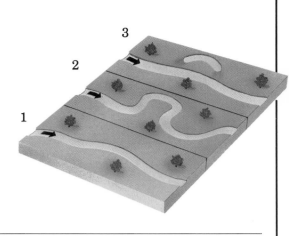

6. Fill a jug with clean, cold water and gently pour some on to the hilly area at the back of the tray. Observe and record what happens, using words and pictures. Describe the path or paths taken by the water. Which materials have been washed into the bowl?

**6**

## BRIGHT IDEAS

Frost action can cause cracks, and stones and bricks may crumble. Fill a screw top glass bottle to the brim with water, and place it inside a sealed plastic bag. Put it into a freezer overnight and you will find that the bottle will break.

Look at the outside of a building. Can you see any signs of weathering? Look up at the roof from each compass direction. Are there any signs of weathering on the ground?

# USING MATERIALS

Natural materials are taken, not only from the Earth, but also from the air, the seas and many plants and animals. Precious metals, like platinum, are extracted from rocks in the Earth, salt is evaporated from the seas, oxygen is separated out from the air, rubber can be tapped from trees, and leather began as the skin of an animal. Cement is a mixture of limestone and clay, and concrete can be made by mixing cement with sand, gravel and water. Gypsum is a soft, non-metallic mineral. It can be found in the Montmartre area of Paris which is why it is sometimes known as Plaster of Paris. The Ancient Egyptians and the Romans used gypsum, which is often called alabaster.

## PLASTER PANSIES

**1**

1. Cut away one side of a soap powder box to make a frame for the mould. Place it on the craft board and seal the edges with waterproof tape. Cover all surfaces, plaster is very messy.

**2**

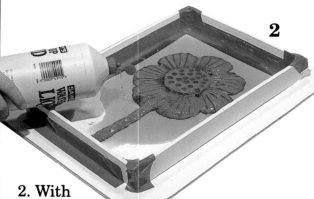

2. With the plasticine, shape a flower inside the frame. Add any extra details with more plasticine. Squeeze washing up liquid all over the finished shape. It will act as a lubricant.

3. Mix the powdered plaster in a bucket with cold water. Stir it quickly, without splashing, to remove any lumps. Try to avoid making air bubbles.

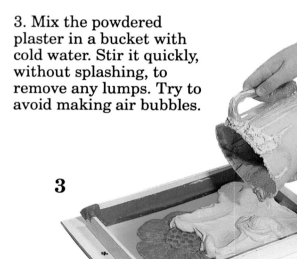

**3**

4. Immediately, pour the mixture over the plasticine flower to fill the frame completely.

**4**

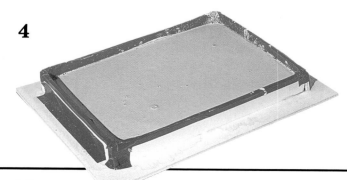

# WHY IT WORKS

Plaster of Paris is made by heating crushed gypsum. When most of the water has been removed, it can be ground to the fine powder. When water is added to Plaster of Paris, a chemical reaction takes place as gypsum is reformed. It sets hard, giving off warmth as the chemical reaction takes place.

Plaster of Paris + Water

= Gypsum

# BRIGHT IDEAS

Use your plaster mould to make flower shapes from plasticine. Press the plasticine into the mould to make an imprint.

Feel the plaster model as it is setting - it will set very quickly and will feel warm. What causes this?

Shape a piece of clay to use as a mould for a plaster model animal. You can paint and varnish your plaster animal.

Use an empty detergent box to make a block of plaster. You can use this to make a sculpture. Carve a shape out of the block.

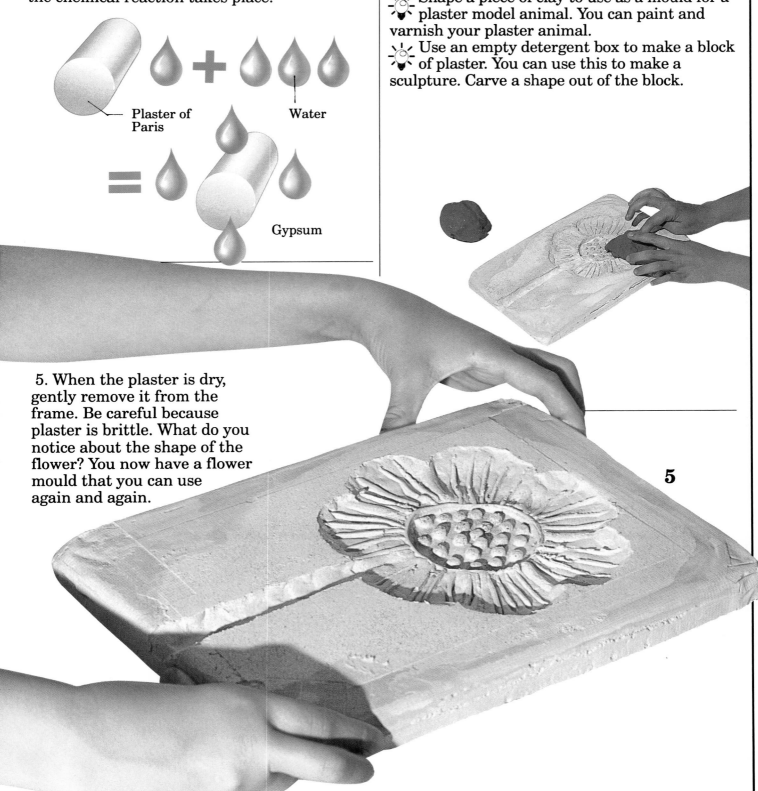

5. When the plaster is dry, gently remove it from the frame. Be careful because plaster is brittle. What do you notice about the shape of the flower? You now have a flower mould that you can use again and again.

5

11

# PROPERTIES OF MATERIALS

Matter is anything that takes up space in the Universe. It may be living or non-living. Every substance and material is made up of small particles called atoms. A material's strength and flexibility depends on the arrangement of its atoms as molecules, and the elasticity of a spring is dependent upon the interaction of these molecules. A spring is either a coil or a bending bar. The suspension in a car depends on springs to provide a smooth ride. A door may have a spring that will return it to a closed position, and tiny springs can be found inside watches. An aeroplane's wings are built of light, flexible materials that allow them to bend and "give" in a strong wind.

## JACK IN THE BOX

**1**

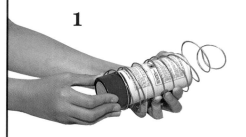

1. Coil some stiff wire into a spring-shape around an empty cylindrical metal container.

**2**

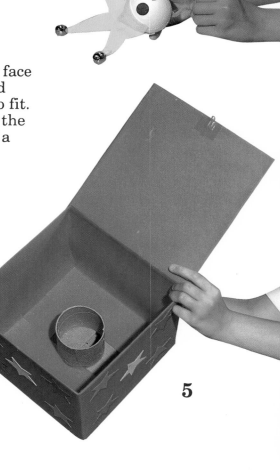

3. The arms and legs are also made from pipe cleaners and the body is a plastic bottle. Cover the bottle with a felt coat. 'Jack' can be anchored to the top of the spring by attaching one end to the bottle lid.

2. Design an interesting face on the ping-pong ball and make a felt jester's hat to fit. Make a hole underneath the head to insert the end of a pipe cleaner.

5. In the bottom of the box attach a ring of cardboard around which the spring should fit snugly. Secure with sticky tape

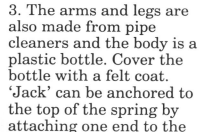

**3**

4. Paint Jack's box and decorate it with attractive stick-on motifs. Paint the inside as well as the outside.

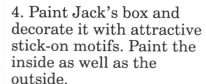

**4**

**5**

# WHY IT WORKS

Most materials have the quality of elasticity, which is the ability to resume their shape after being bent or pulled by an outside force. Metals can be made to have more stretch by bending them into a spring. In a spring at rest, the attracting and repelling forces between its molecules are balanced (1). Squeezing the spring increases the repelling forces, releasing the spring pushes the molecules apart again (2).

Molecule

Repelling forces

Attracting forces

# BRIGHT IDEAS

Hang a weight from a ruler and hold it over the edge of a table. Leave about 5 cm sticking out, and watch how far it bends. Now move the ruler further out over the edge. Does it bend further? Try using rulers of wood, plastic and metal. Which is the most flexible?

6. Attach the back of Jack's coat to the lid of the box so that he will stand upright when the lid is lifted. Secure the lid closed with a pin.

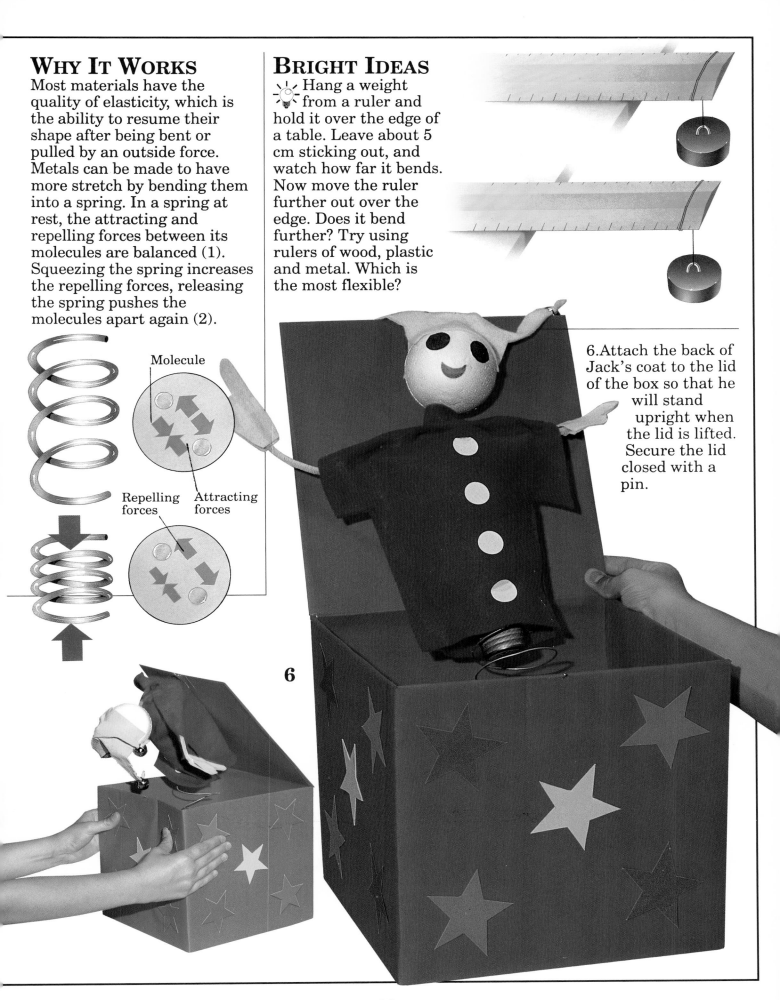

6

# MAKING NEW MATERIALS

The properties of a material help determine its use. Physical properties, such as mass and volume can be measured, but it is also important to know how a material behaves or responds to treatment. Sometimes it is possible to change the properties of one material by combining it with another. Raw materials that are chemically changed into another substance are called synthetic, or man-made, materials. Heat is often required to cause a chemical change. Bronze is a hard strong alloy (mixture) of copper, tin and other metals. Adding phosphorous hardens and strengthens bronze. Bronze is the oldest alloy known.

## PETRIFIED PAPER

**1**

3. To shape the base rest the balloon inside a wide plastic lid and stick the paste strips over the plastic. Shape two handles from folded strips of papier mâché and fix them in position with more strips.

**3**

1. Using flour and water or wallpaper paste, make a mixture that has a runny consistency but is thicker than water. Tear or cut some newspapers into even sized strips. Soak each strip thoroughly in the paste.

4. The finished shape must be left to dry out completely before the balloon is removed. The bowl can then be painted and varnished.

**4**

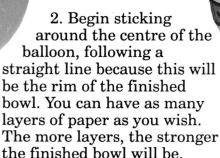

**2**

2. Begin sticking around the centre of the balloon, following a straight line because this will be the rim of the finished bowl. You can have as many layers of paper as you wish. The more layers, the stronger the finished bowl will be.

# WHY IT WORKS

Each material has its own structure of molecules. In a solid, the molecules are packed closely together. In a liquid, the molecules move around more easily, and in a gas they move around very quickly. Adhesion is what causes two substances to stick together. A liquid (like the flour and water paste),can fill all the holes on the surface of the paper and then set hard, forming a bond.

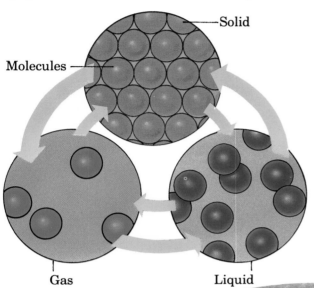

Molecules

Solid

Gas

Liquid

# BRIGHT IDEAS

💡 Use a variety of materials to weave together.
💡 Choose contrasting materials for the warp and weft threads (below), such as string and wool or grasses and twigs. How strong is the new "fabric".
💡 Use single sheets of newspaper dipped in paste and lie them on top of each other in layers until you have a 'block' of papier mâché. Cut a shape out of the block or mould over a large shape, and leave to dry.
💡 Cut strips of paper dipped in paste and wind them round a 'ball' of newspaper. Make a clay mould, brush with soapy water, and fill with the pulp mixture.

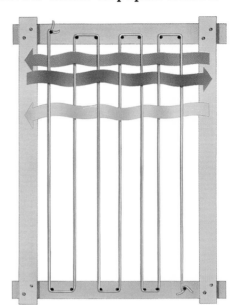

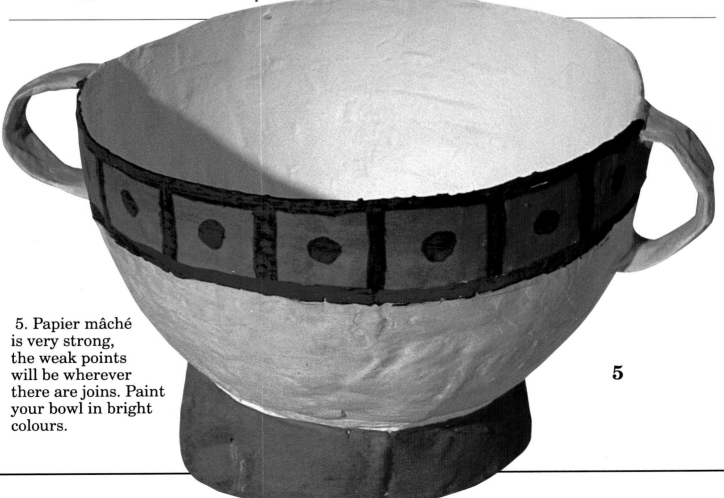

5. Papier mâché is very strong, the weak points will be wherever there are joins. Paint your bowl in bright colours.

**5**

# CHOOSING MATERIALS

It's very important to choose the best material for certain jobs. Metals are good conductors of heat. In contrast, wood is a poor conductor of heat, but is a good insulator. In our daily lives, we use metal saucepans to conduct heat during the cooking process, but we also need to protect ourselves from burning by using heat-proof oven gloves. Space-craft have heat shields that protect them from the high temperature caused by friction during re-entry through the atmosphere. The Space Shuttle, has heat resistant tiles. 30,000 tiles made from silica fibre must be fitted individually.

## MELT DOWN!

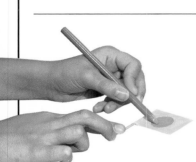

1. Cut out three small paper flags, decorate each with a different motif and attach them to cocktail sticks like this. Now cut out three identical pieces of cooking fat.

**1**

2. Take one metal and one plastic lid. Place one piece of fat on each of the lids.

**2**

Now cut a piece of cork of similar thickness. Push a flag into each piece of fat.

4. Use a watch with a second hand to time how long it takes for each flag to fall. The flags will fall as the fat melts. The heat from the water will travel through the materials at different speeds.

**3**

3. Half fill the plastic bowl with clean, hot water. Do not use boiling water. When the surface is still, position each lid on the water, making sure that you keep a record of the precise time that each lid touches the hot surface.

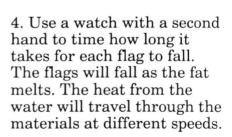

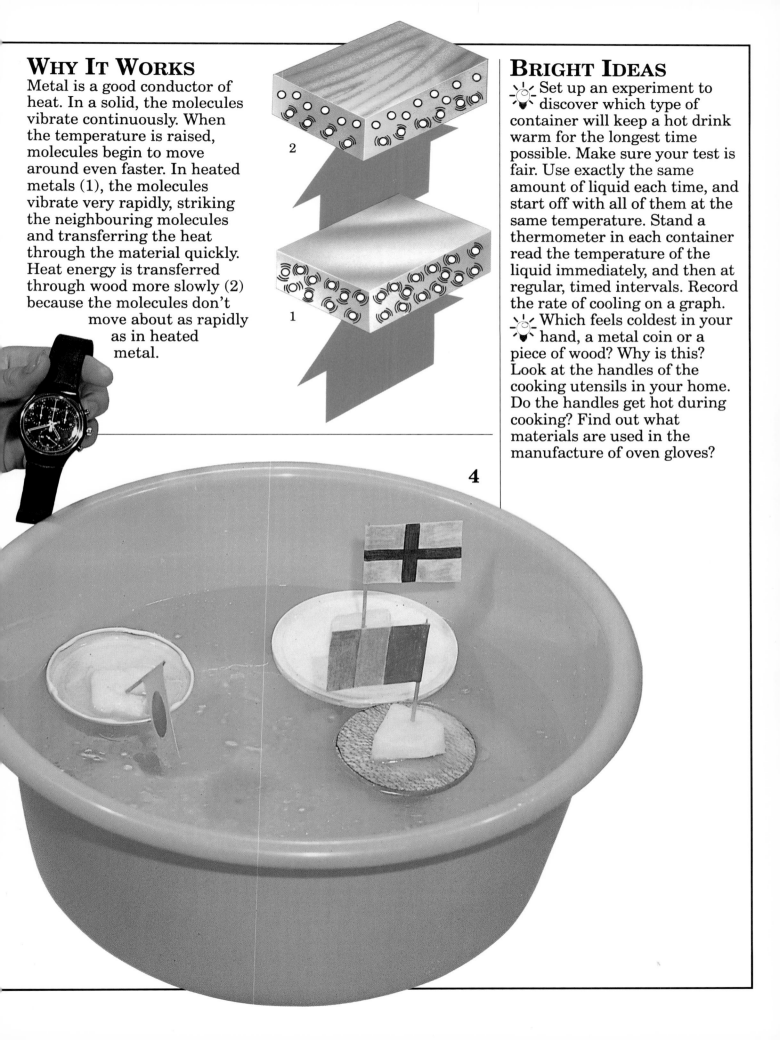

## WHY IT WORKS
Metal is a good conductor of heat. In a solid, the molecules vibrate continuously. When the temperature is raised, molecules begin to move around even faster. In heated metals (1), the molecules vibrate very rapidly, striking the neighbouring molecules and transferring the heat through the material quickly. Heat energy is transferred through wood more slowly (2) because the molecules don't move about as rapidly as in heated metal.

2

1

## BRIGHT IDEAS
Set up an experiment to discover which type of container will keep a hot drink warm for the longest time possible. Make sure your test is fair. Use exactly the same amount of liquid each time, and start off with all of them at the same temperature. Stand a thermometer in each container read the temperature of the liquid immediately, and then at regular, timed intervals. Record the rate of cooling on a graph.

Which feels coldest in your hand, a metal coin or a piece of wood? Why is this? Look at the handles of the cooking utensils in your home. Do the handles get hot during cooking? Find out what materials are used in the manufacture of oven gloves?

4

# SHAPES IN NATURE

The smallest unit of living matter is the cell, which is able to divide and multiply. A plant cell has a rigid wall of cellulose, that gives it structure and shape. An animal cell is surrounded only by a thin membrane, so some animals (vertebrates) need a bony skeleton. Some invertebrates, like the crab, have an exoskeleton (an outer skeleton that protects the soft inner body). Nature has developed many strong structures. A honeycomb is a strong structure of hexagonal cells that fit snugly, side by side, without any overlapping or gaps. This is called a tesselated structure.

## TOUGH TESSELLATION

1. To make this tessellation game, you will need coloured card. Use a stencil to cut out hexagon-shaped counters in 2 colours. They should be the same size.

**1**

2. Use the yellow card for the honeycomb design on the board. Trace the tessellated hexagons so that you have a total of 60.

**2**

4. There should be alternate rows of 7 and 8 hexagons. Emphasise the divisions by going over them with a black felt tip pen.

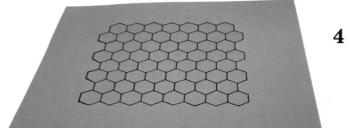

**4**

3. Carefully cut round the outside of the yellow honeycomb and position it centrally on more card.

**3**

5. Draw the net for a large cube on white card and construct a die with it. With a marker pen, put the digits 1 and 2 on the sides of the die so that there are 3 of each.

**5**

# WHY IT WORKS

The complex structure of a honeycomb is a series of six-sided wax cells. Any weight on one cell in the comb is spread out over 3 cells below and 5 cells below that. Tessellating squares rest on only 1 or 2 half squares. Because regular hexagons tessellate (there are no gaps and no overlaps) less space is wasted. A six-sided framework is stronger than a square but not as strong as a circle. Circles, however, cannot be tessellated. There would be gaps left between them.

# BRIGHT IDEAS

- Follow the pattern below and create a spiral using nails and wool. Each point on the curve should be joined to every other point.
- Look closely at a snail shell and the horns of a sheep. Do they all curl in the same direction?
- Try creating a variety of tessellations using squares or equilateral triangles. You can design repeating patterns.

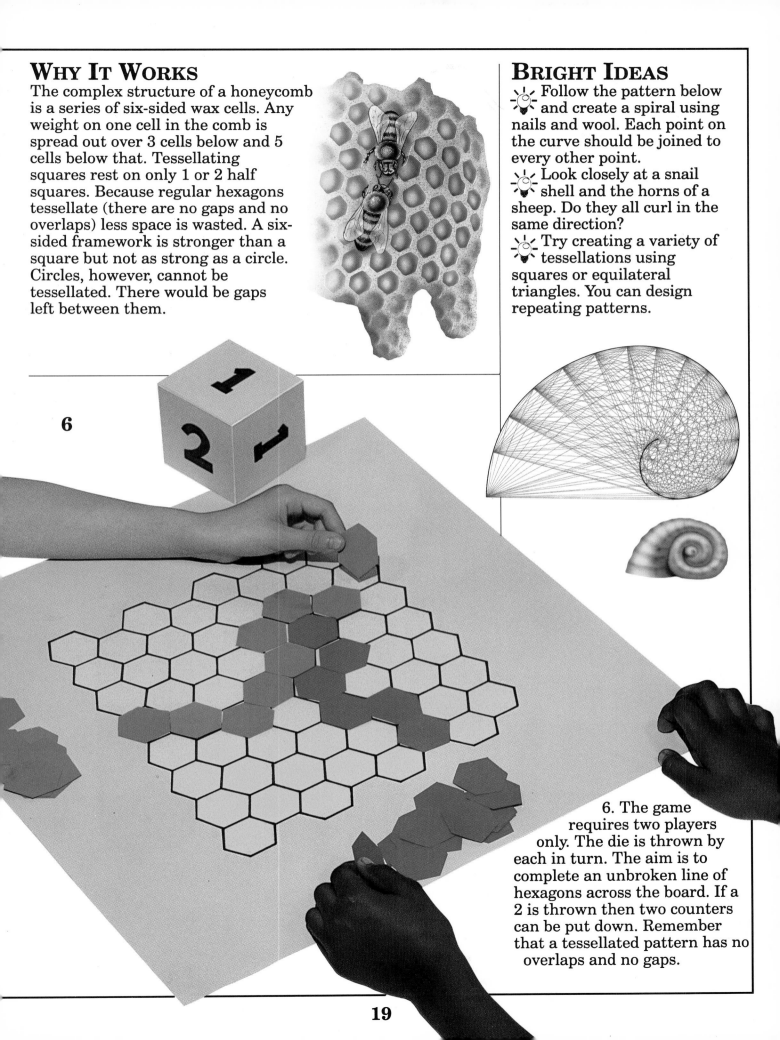

6. The game requires two players only. The die is thrown by each in turn. The aim is to complete an unbroken line of hexagons across the board. If a 2 is thrown then two counters can be put down. Remember that a tessellated pattern has no overlaps and no gaps.

# STRONG SHAPES

Certain structures, natural and man-made, are stronger than others. The absence of corners in round shapes, or spheres can be a source of strength, because pressure is spread around the whole surface. Domes like this one in St. Paul's Cathedral, London provide a strong ceiling to a building. The geodesic dome (left) was created by Robert Buckminster-Fuller. It is a strong, self-supporting structure. His original design had a framework of hexagons and pentagons, like some footballs. Transparent 'bubble' domes are now supplied as a standard system of steel cables and rods that support triangular sheets of glass.

## STRONG SHAPES

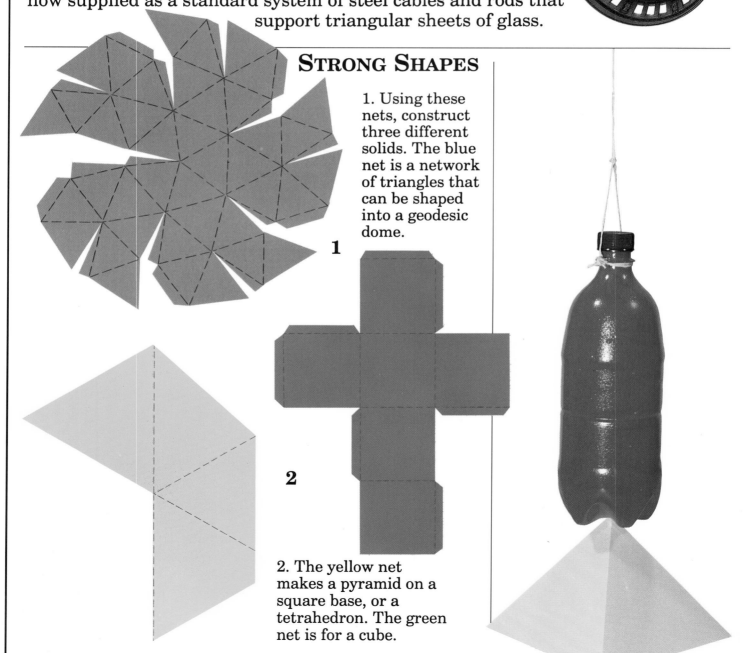

1. Using these nets, construct three different solids. The blue net is a network of triangles that can be shaped into a geodesic dome.

**1**

**2**

2. The yellow net makes a pyramid on a square base, or a tetrahedron. The green net is for a cube.

## WHY IT WORKS

It is important to be aware of the effect of external forces on a structure. The spherical shape of the geodesic dome reduces the amount of stress in one particular area, and spreads pressure evenly over the whole surface. The triangular framework helps to even out any pressure on the shape and gives the structure rigidity. Hollow tubes combine great strength with light weight. A tube is equally strong all around.

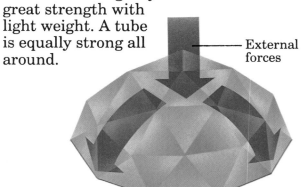

External forces

## BRIGHT IDEAS

☀️ Construct a geodesic dome from plastic straws. You can join the straws as shown here using pins and small pieces of foam rubber. Will it bear more weight than a cube or a pyramid made from straws?

☀️ Design a structure from short lengths of a rigid material like wood, that will support a given weight. Start with a basic cube frame. How can you strengthen it? Try using extra thicknesses of material. Triangulating the frame will make it even stronger (see page 23).

3. Use the same method to join the edges together on each shape and try to keep the sizes proportionate. All of these factors will help ensure a fair test. Fill a plastic bottle with sand, to act as a weight, and suspend it above the first shape. You are testing the efficiency of each solid structure to withstand an external force.

4. The same weight must be used on each solid. Devise a pulley system to ensure that the same force is applied each time. Which shape withstands the external force best? Does it continue to do so over a given length of time? Keep an accurate record of your results.

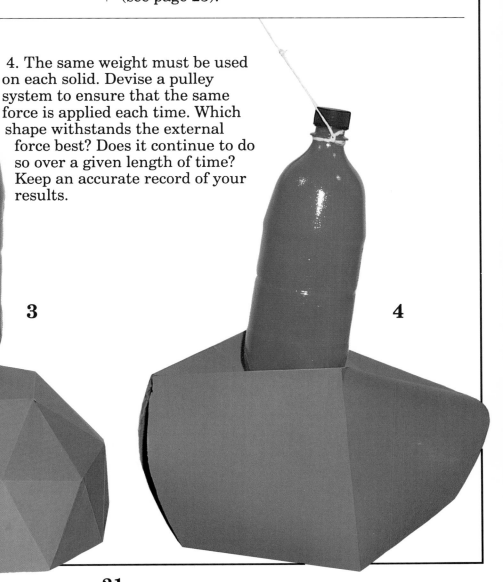

3

4

# RIGID STRUCTURES

The human elbow joint works like a hinge. Joints work with the help of muscles fixed to the bones by tendons. Like the skeleton of a human-being or any other animal, cranes have to be light, manoeuvrable, strong and very sturdy. Cranes are vital in the building of large structures, and they are usually built from a steel framework of thin girders. Without cranes, the building of the Great Pyramid at Giza took 100,000 men, 20 years to complete. The crane has a moveable arm, or jib, that operates by combining the principles of levers and pulleys.

## STRENGTH AND MOVEMENT

**1**

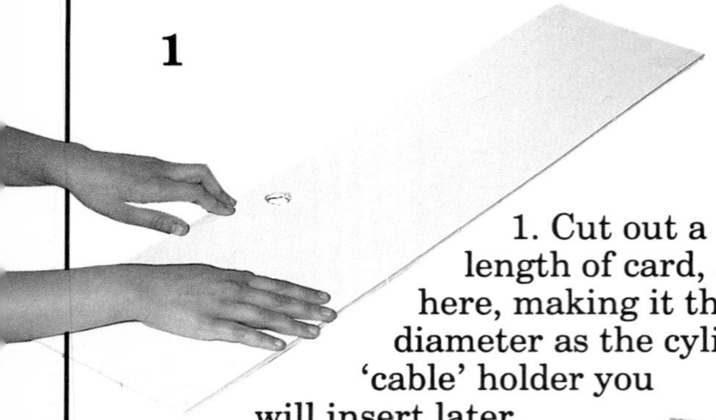

1. Cut out a hole in a length of card, as shown here, making it the same diameter as the cylindrical 'cable' holder you will insert later.

**2**

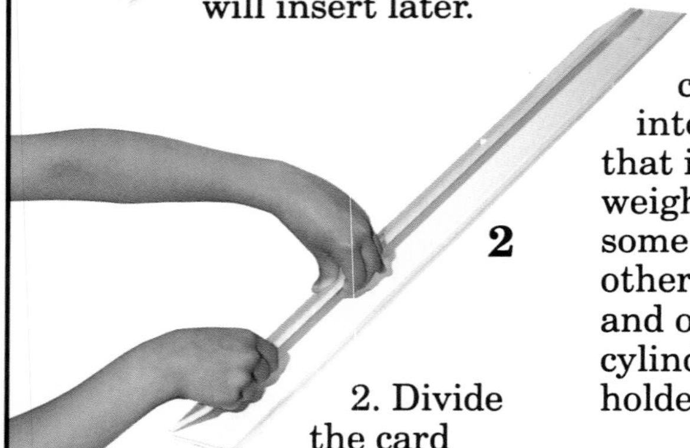

2. Divide the card lengthways into three and score along the lines. Fold to make the elongated prism shape of the jib or 'arm'. Glue the edges.

**3**

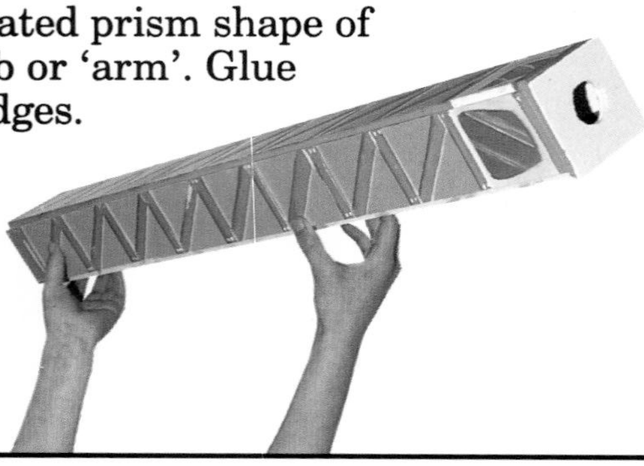

3. In one end of an aluminium foil container, cut out a hole as shown. Glue down any open edges and decorate to look like the body of a real crane.

**4**

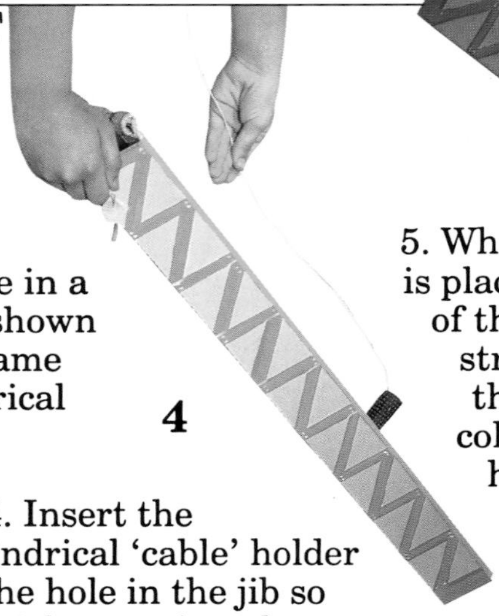

4. Insert the cylindrical 'cable' holder into the hole in the jib so that it sticks out. Attach a weighted hook to one end of some string and thread the other end through the arm and out through the cylindrical holder.

**5**

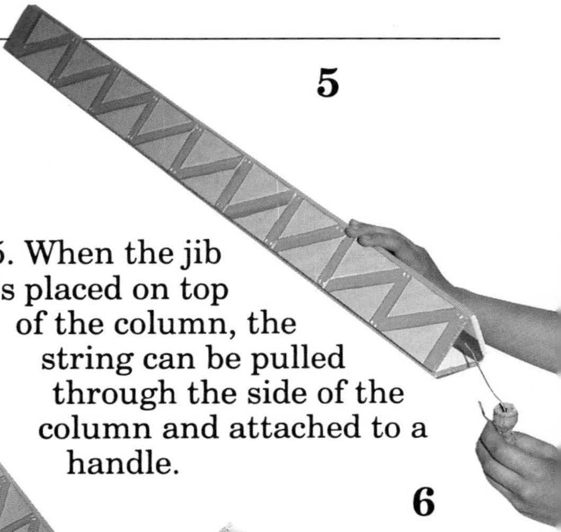

5. When the jib is placed on top of the column, the string can be pulled through the side of the column and attached to a handle.

**6**

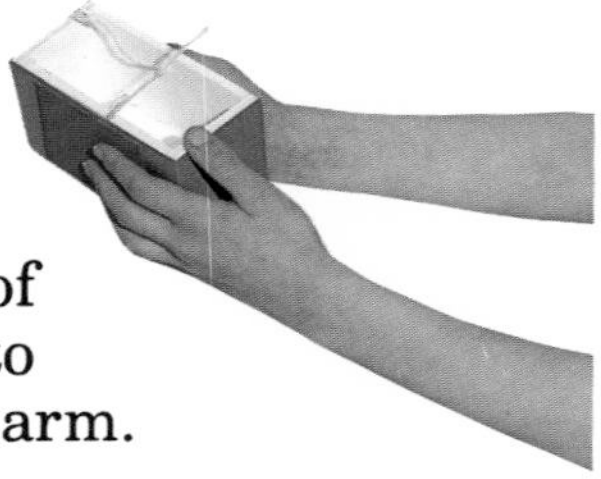

6. Make a ballast box of thick card to balance the arm.

**7**

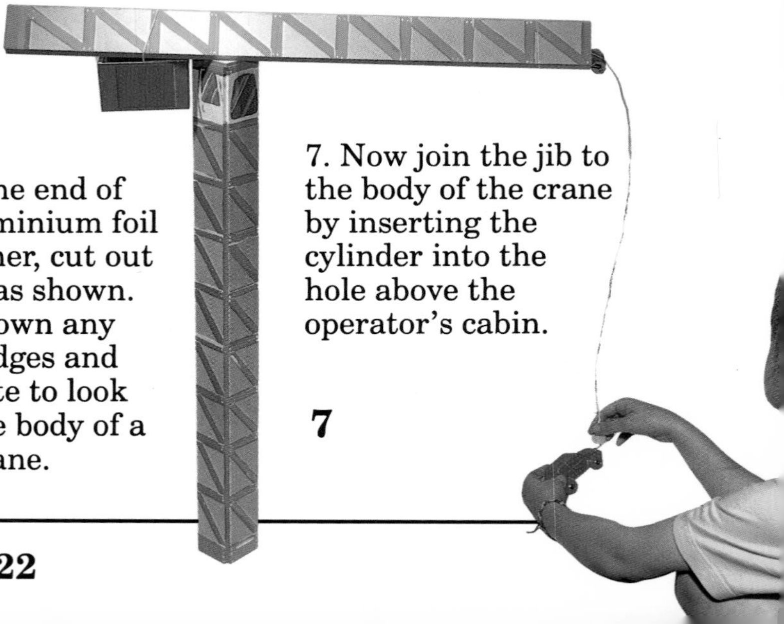

7. Now join the jib to the body of the crane by inserting the cylinder into the hole above the operator's cabin.

**8**

8. Decorate the small ballast box and attach it to the jib so it can slide along. You could weight it with plasticine.

Lower the weighted hook and attach a load. If the crane should lose balance, move the ballast box to compensate.

## WHY IT WORKS

In order to maintain the shape of the structure, internal and external forces must balance. Each part of a structure is called a member. They are either under tension (a pulling force) when they are called "ties", or under compression (a pressing force) when they are called "struts." If pressed from both sides, for example at a join, the pressing force is called "shear". Triangulation produces a stable structure, because a triangle is a more rigid shape than a square. A real crane is therefore constructed from a series of triangles (below left) to prevent movement of the joints (below right).

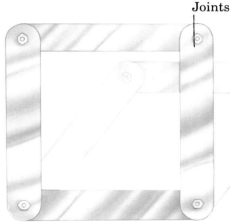

Joints

## BRIGHT IDEAS

Construct a model arm from cardboard strips joined together with paper fasteners. Attach elastic bands to the paper fasteners so that they lengthen and shorten, like real muscles, when the 'arm' moves up and down.

Can you build a crane with a jib that moves from side to side as well as up and down? Is your crane stable? Try making the area of the base larger. Does your crane need more ballast, to balance against the weight of the load?

Why are triangular struts successful? Find other ways of constructing a rigid structure. Join 4 plastic straws, the same length, with thread, to form a square. Is it rigid? Now remove one straw to form a triangle. Is this shape rigid?

# BUILDING TOWERS

Lewis Mumford, the American city-planning historian, wrote in 1938, "The age of crustacean building has given way to the age of vertebrates, and the wall, no longer a protective shell, has become a skin." He was referring to the revolution in high-rise building that was brought about by the introduction of iron or steel frames to take the strain in buildings. Shell structures were replaced by frame stuctures. Load-bearing walls no longer limited the height of buildings, and the first skyscrapers made their appearance. The high-rise, steel frame was developed by William le Baron Jenney. The Canadian National Tower in Toronto is 553m high.

## REACH FOR THE SKY

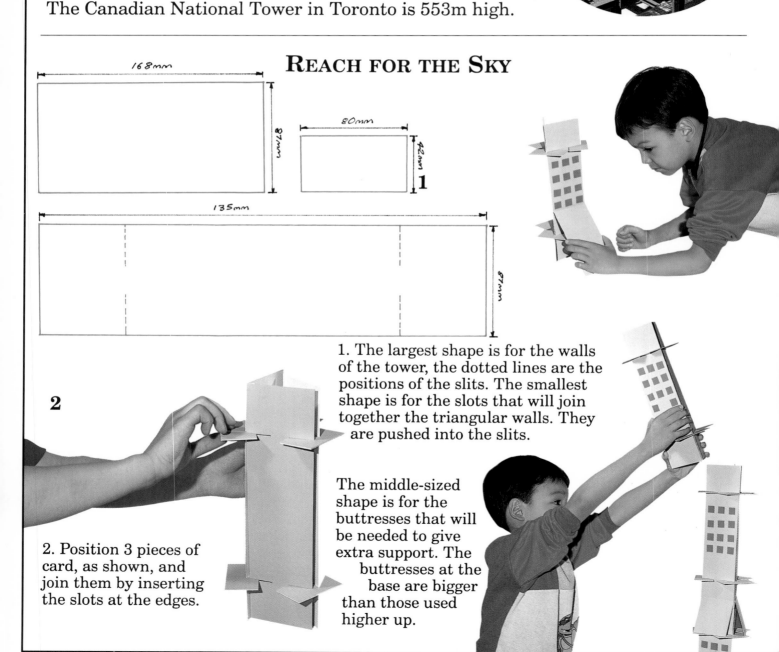

1. The largest shape is for the walls of the tower, the dotted lines are the positions of the slits. The smallest shape is for the slots that will join together the triangular walls. They are pushed into the slits.

2. Position 3 pieces of card, as shown, and join them by inserting the slots at the edges.

The middle-sized shape is for the buttresses that will be needed to give extra support. The buttresses at the base are bigger than those used higher up.

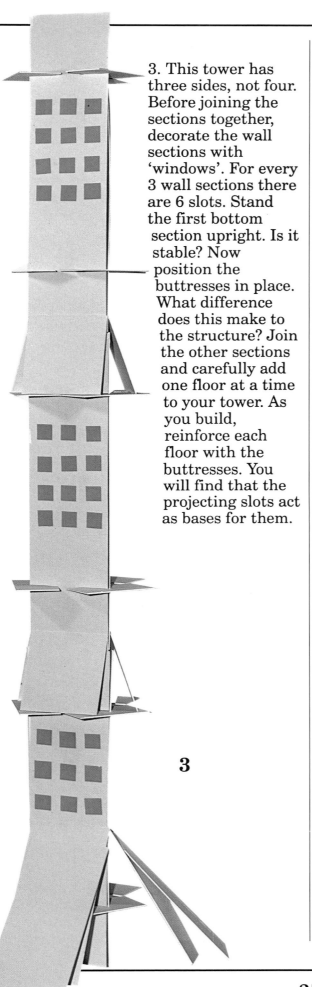

3. This tower has three sides, not four. Before joining the sections together, decorate the wall sections with 'windows'. For every 3 wall sections there are 6 slots. Stand the first bottom section upright. Is it stable? Now position the buttresses in place. What difference does this make to the structure? Join the other sections and carefully add one floor at a time to your tower. As you build, reinforce each floor with the buttresses. You will find that the projecting slots act as bases for them.

3

## WHY IT WORKS

Your tower structure has stability because it has buttresses that stick out to give support in the form of a broad base, instead of foundations. The forces that the tower exerts downwards are balanced by the buttresses which exert another force upwards from the ground. The higher you build your tower the less stability it will have, and the greater the support it will need. A skyscraper built around a framework, must have foundations that support the weight of the structure - it must be stable, but flexible in high winds.

Downward forces

Upward forces

## BRIGHT IDEAS

Roll a piece of stiff paper into a tube shape and fix it with sticky tape. How strong do you think this shape is? See how many books you can balance on the top.

How high can you build your tower before it overbalances? Will it withstand a 'wind'? Try using a hair dryer to test it. Is it rigid or flexible?

Now try slotting together shapes to make a four-sided tower. Is it more stable than your three-sided structure?

What happens when you build a shell structure, like a tower of bricks? Why do you think it is unstable? How can you give it stability? Try building a tower framework out of plastic straws and pipecleaners, or artstraws.

# SUSPENDED STRUCTURES

The first bridge was probably a fallen tree laid across a stream and early bridge-builders may have observed the strength of rock arches, carved by natural forces. There are 3 types of bridge – arch, girder and suspension. Each one displaces its weight differently. The Golden Gate Bridge, in San Francisco (left), completed in 1937, is a suspension bridge with a main span of 1280m. The Humber Bridge is the world's longest single span suspension bridge. It has a span of 1410m. The newest type of bridge is the cable-stayed, a design related to the suspension bridge but the cables are connected directly to the towers.

## CROSS THE RIVER

1. For this project you will need a large board as a base. On the board, paint a river scene like the one shown here. Use a craft board and carefully cut 6 polystyrene sections for the roadway of the bridge. You will need a large ball of strong string because the 'cables' carry the weight of the roadway.

**1**

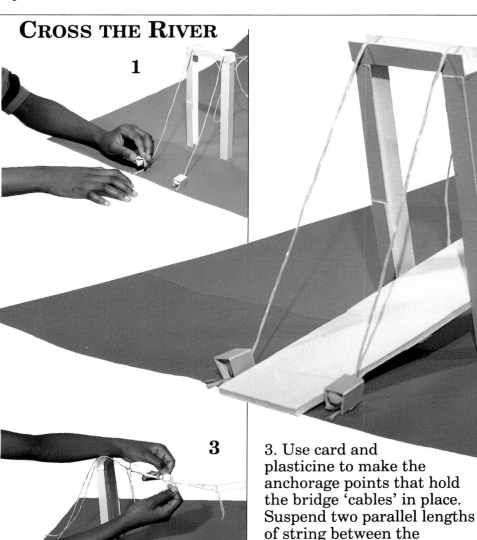

**2**

2. Cut 10 of the smaller shapes out of stiff card. Measure and mark the scoring lines. Score and fold along the lines to make the tower sections. Glue 2 sections together to form the sides of each tower and use one section as a cross beam. Glue the finished towers firmly to the board. Make sure that they are directly opposite each other, on either side of the river.

**3**

3. Use card and plasticine to make the anchorage points that hold the bridge 'cables' in place. Suspend two parallel lengths of string between the anchorage points as shown. Make the supports for the roadway by knotting loops of string between the cables.

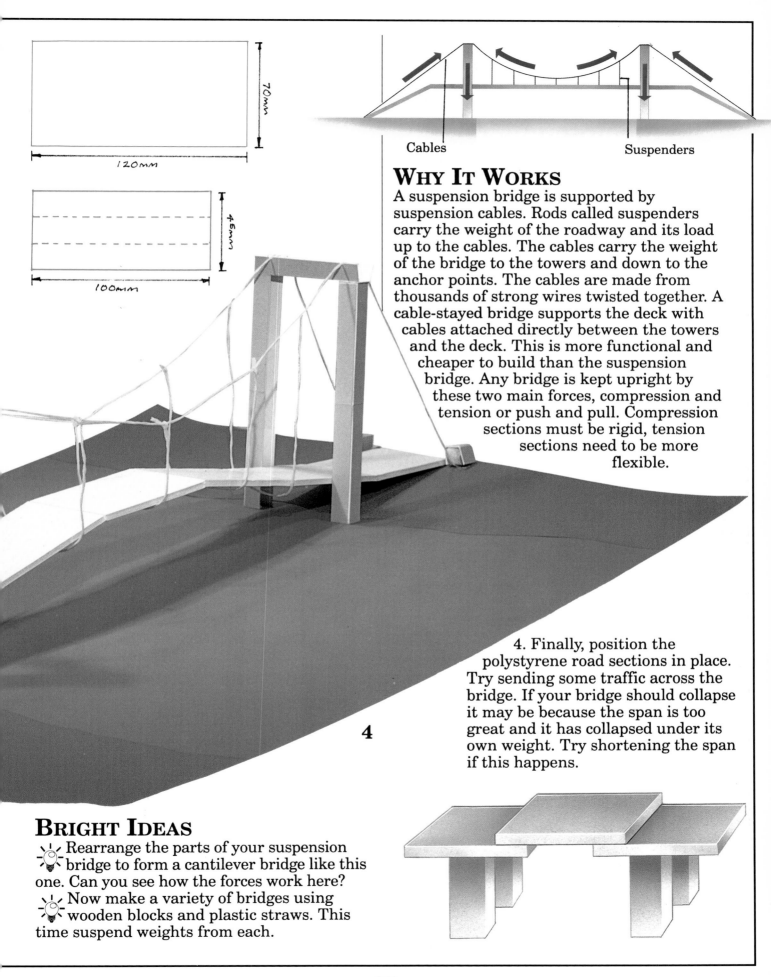

120mm

70mm

100mm

45mm

Cables

Suspenders

## WHY IT WORKS

A suspension bridge is supported by suspension cables. Rods called suspenders carry the weight of the roadway and its load up to the cables. The cables carry the weight of the bridge to the towers and down to the anchor points. The cables are made from thousands of strong wires twisted together. A cable-stayed bridge supports the deck with cables attached directly between the towers and the deck. This is more functional and cheaper to build than the suspension bridge. Any bridge is kept upright by these two main forces, compression and tension or push and pull. Compression sections must be rigid, tension sections need to be more flexible.

4

4. Finally, position the polystyrene road sections in place. Try sending some traffic across the bridge. If your bridge should collapse it may be because the span is too great and it has collapsed under its own weight. Try shortening the span if this happens.

## BRIGHT IDEAS

Rearrange the parts of your suspension bridge to form a cantilever bridge like this one. Can you see how the forces work here?

Now make a variety of bridges using wooden blocks and plastic straws. This time suspend weights from each.

# COMBINING MATERIALS

It is possible to combine materials in such a way that the final substance retains the best properties of each. Fibreglass, for example, is glass-reinforced plastic which is light, flexible yet strong. These are known as composite materials. The idea is not a new one. Homes built from wattle and daub were being constructed hundreds of years ago. The first bricks were a mixture of clay and straw. The Inuit eskimos froze moss into ice to strengthen their dome-shaped igloos, constructed using a spiral structure. Today, concrete is reinforced with steel rods (above). Nature has its own composite materials, like wood and bone, both of which are strong but light.

## TEST YOUR STRENGTH!

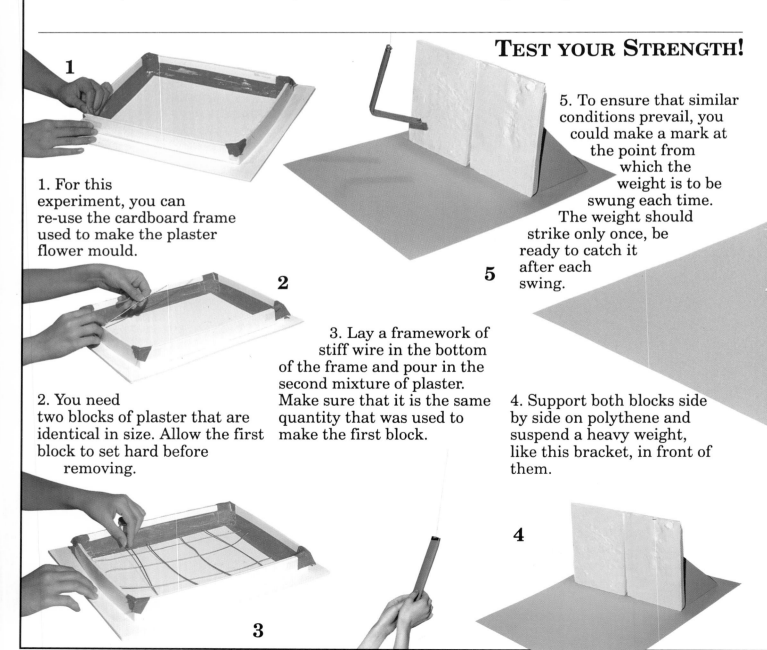

1. For this experiment, you can re-use the cardboard frame used to make the plaster flower mould.

2. You need two blocks of plaster that are identical in size. Allow the first block to set hard before removing.

3. Lay a framework of stiff wire in the bottom of the frame and pour in the second mixture of plaster. Make sure that it is the same quantity that was used to make the first block.

4. Support both blocks side by side on polythene and suspend a heavy weight, like this bracket, in front of them.

5. To ensure that similar conditions prevail, you could make a mark at the point from which the weight is to be swung each time. The weight should strike only once, be ready to catch it after each swing.

# WHY IT WORKS

The brittle plaster block breaks easily when an external force is applied (1). The plaster and wire block is able to withstand a greater force because it has been re-inforced with the strength of the wire (2). A composite material has better mechanical properties than any of its components. These materials can be incorporated as fibres in a weaker material, called the matrix. The matrix bonds with and holds the fibres together.

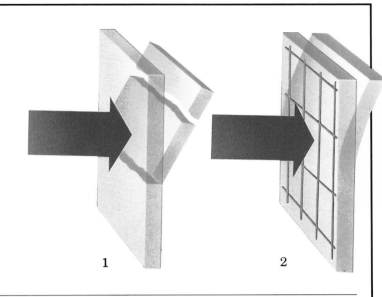

1                                    2

# BRIGHT IDEAS

Shape bricks out of clay and leave them to harden. Now shape bricks mixed with straw and allow them to harden. Test them for strength by tapping them with a hammer. Be careful, wear protective glasses. Which are the strongest?

**6**

6. Eventually both blocks will crack. How many swings of the weight are needed before this happens? Draw conclusions from your observations. The best properties of the wire and the plaster have been combined in the composite

# VERSATILE STRUCTURES

Kites are named after a bird that has a ragged, flapping flight, interspersed with soaring. The Chinese saw kite-flying as an art form, as long ago as the 4th century BC. The framework was lashed bamboo, covered with silk or paper. It was not until the 16th century that kites reached Europe. Kites have been used for scientific experiments, military signalling and religious festivals. Handgliders (left) are large kites with very rigid, aluminium structures.

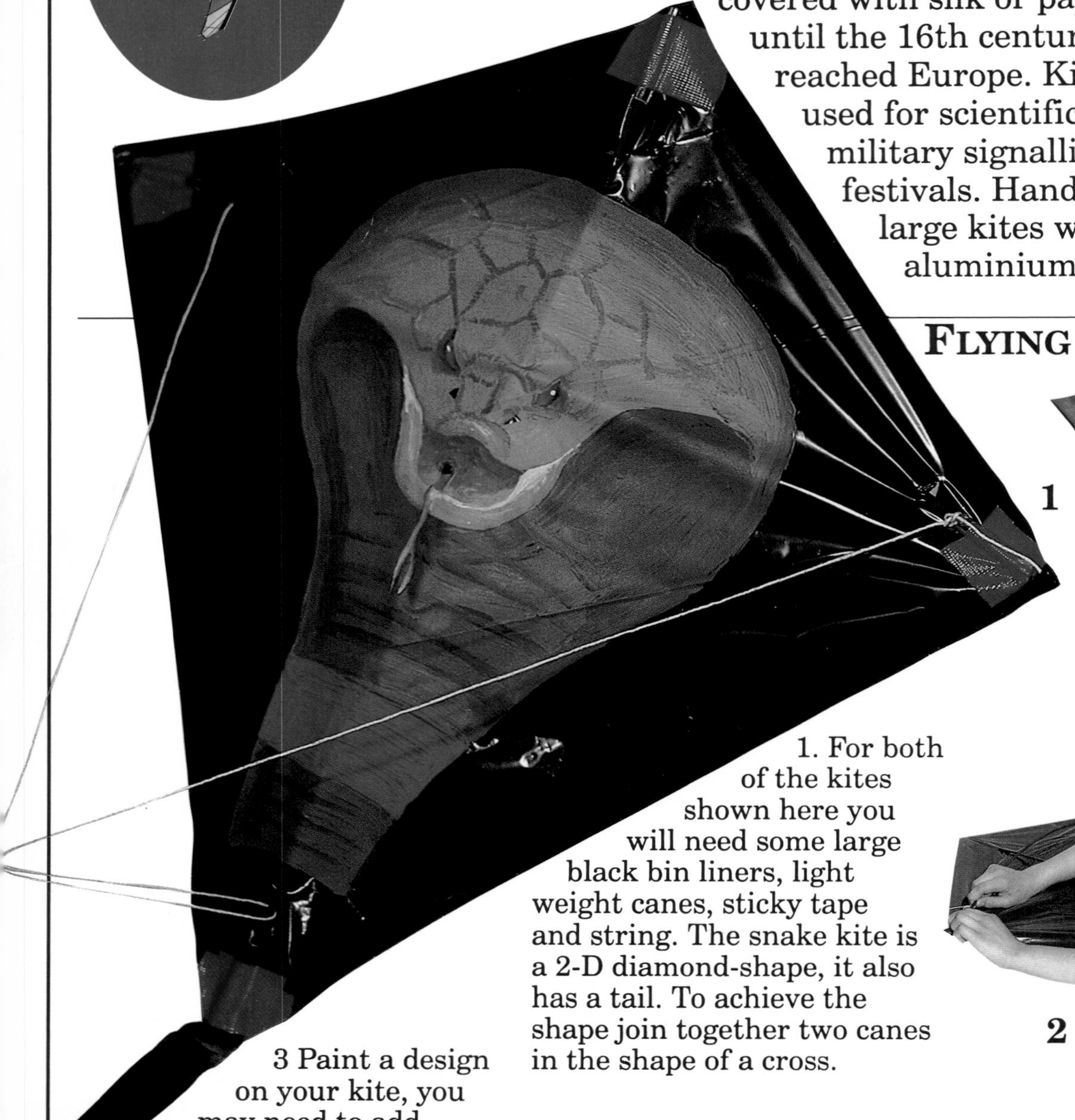

## FLYING HIGH!

**1**

1. For both of the kites shown here you will need some large black bin liners, light weight canes, sticky tape and string. The snake kite is a 2-D diamond-shape, it also has a tail. To achieve the shape join together two canes in the shape of a cross.

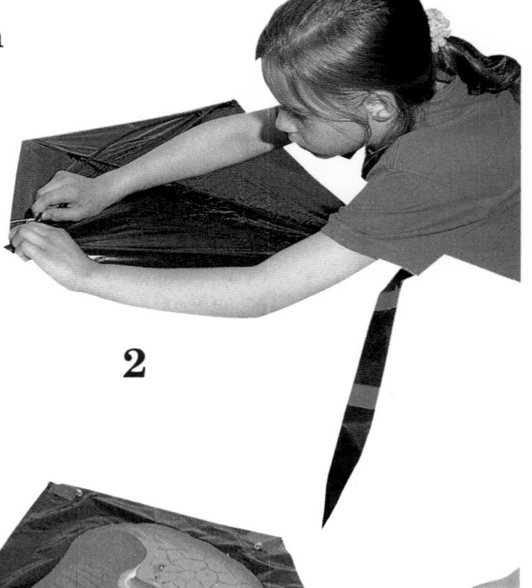

**2**

3 Paint a design on your kite, you may need to add some paste to the paint because the surface is shiny. Try sticking on self-adhesive motifs.

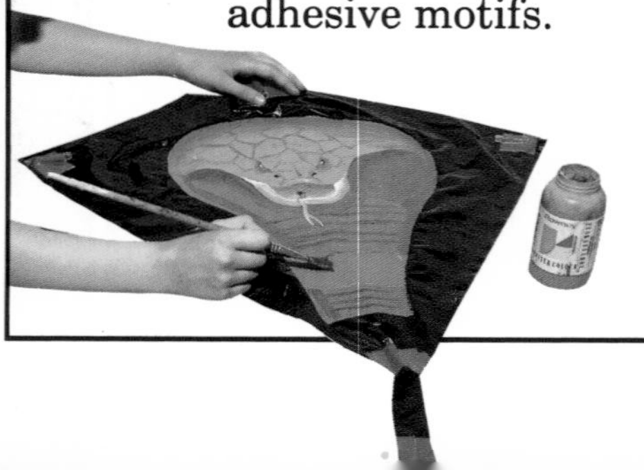

2. Fix a pen lid to each corner of the kite with strong tape. These will enable you to insert the ends of your canes, threading them through from the opposite side.

**3**

**4.** Secure the canes at the back and front with more strong tape and join together long, thin sections of plastic to make a tail. The tail needs to be about 40 cm long.

**4**

**6**

**6.** The second kite is quite different because it is 3-D. It is a triangular box kite. The framework is made from strong but light canes. Join the canes as shown here with strong stick-tape. Large, black plastic bin liners have again been used. They will have to be cut into lengths that can be wrapped around the cane framework.

**7.** Decorate the plastic before attaching it to the frame. Make sure your frame is securely held together with sticky tape. It will need to be sturdy enough to fly in a strong wind.

**7**

**5.** Tie the string to 3 corners of the kite, as shown, fixing it to the cane itself. Now attach the handling string which must be very long. The longer your string is, the higher you can fly your kite.

**5**

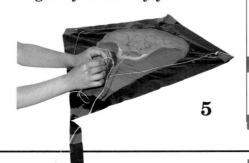

**1**

**2**

## WHY IT WORKS

The flat kite has a tail to give it direction, the bowed kite is curved at an angle to the wind. Box kites are 3-D, the delta is triangular and the flexible kite or parafoil forms its shape when filled by the wind. The wind moves past the kite to cause a force called lift which makes it rise. The forces of lift, drag and gravity combine to keep the kite in the air. When the kite is flown in such a way that its angle against the wind (angle of attack) provides maximum lift, drag and gravity are overcome (1). The angle is controlled by the short lines called bridles (2).

# SCIENTIFIC TERMS

**BALLAST** A heavy material used to supply weight or stability.

**BRITTLE** Easily cracked or broken; fragile.

**CAVITY WALL** Two walls built with a space between.

**CELLULOSE** The main constituent of a plant cell.

**EROSION** The wearing away of a material by the action of weathering or a substance such as water.

**EVAPORATION** Loss of water to the atmosphere.

**EQUILIBRIUM** The state of being balanced.

**FLEXIBLE** Can be bent easily without breaking.

**GYPSUM** A mineral from the ground that can be heated to form Plaster of Paris.

**IGNEOUS** Rocks derived from magma or lava, on or below Earth's surface.

**INVERTABRATE** An animal without a backbone, but with an outer shell, such as a crab.

**MAGMA** Hot liquid beneath Earth's crust that solidifies into igneous rock.

**MEMBRANE** A pliable tissue that connects cells and organs.

**STABILIZER** A device used to achieve stability.

**TENSILE STRENGTH** The ability of a material to withstand a pulling force.

**VARIABLE** An aspect of change in an experiment.

**VERTABRATE** An animal with a backbone.

---

# INDEX